Usborne

Little First Stickers

Aquarium

Illustrated by Marcella Grassi

Words by Hannah Watson

Designed by Yasmin Faulkner

Expert advice from Dr. John Rostron
and Dr. Margaret Rostron

You'll find all the
stickers at the back
of the book.

Coral reef

Beautiful coral reefs are the perfect home for all kinds of tropical fish. Corals may look like plants, but they are really animals.

Find a place for a butterflyfish.

Add lots of little clownfish.

Open ocean

Add a green sea turtle gliding gracefully through the water. This turtle can hold its breath for five hours.

Stick on a shoal of squirrelfish swimming by.

Find a space for lots
of unicorn tangs.

Stick on some snappers
with electric blue stripes.

Sharks

Sharks patrol the sandy floor and explore rocky caves as golden trevallies swim peacefully by.

Add a blacktip reef shark swimming into this cave.

Find a place for a grey reef shark.

Stick on some more
nurse sharks.

Penguin pool

These gentoo penguins waddle across the ice and chase each other through the water.

Add a penguin feeding her chick.

Fill the water with playful penguins.

Rainforest river

Piranhas weave through the tall river weeds. Though people often think they are dangerous, these piranhas usually just eat insects and plants.

Find a place for a couple of catfish.

Add some bright
tetras darting along.

In a rockpool

Rockpools are home to amazing
sea anemones, spiny sea urchins
and pretty starfish.

Find a place for a sea anemone.

Stick on a
sea urchin.

Seahorses and seadragons

Seahorses use their tails to cling on to swaying reeds, while seadragons float past.

Find a place for a weedy seadragon.

Add some seahorses resting by these plants.

Ray lagoon

Add some rays skimming along the floor,
and some more plaice resting on the sand.

Add two more dogfish
to the lagoon.

Stick on lots of
ray egg cases.

Find a bright blue cuckoo
wrasse to stick on.

Lots of jellyfish

These pacific sea nettle jellyfish use their long stinging tentacles to capture food.

Fill this tank with jellyfish swimming in all directions.